For Becca

First Edition   1 2 3 4 5 6 7 8 9 10

Library of Congress Cataloging in Publication Data

McMillan, Bruce.   Becca backward, Becca frontward: a book of concept pairs.

Summary: Photographs of a girl involved in various activities illustrate such opposite concepts as above/below, full/empty, and big/small.   1. English language—Synonyms and antonyms—Juvenile literature. [1. English language—Synonyms and antonyms]

I. Title.   PE1591.M43   1986   428.1   86-7221

ISBN 0-688-06282-2   ISBN 0-688-06283-0 (lib. bdg.)

Becca Backward, Becca Frontward

A BOOK OF CONCEPT PAIRS

BRUCE McMILLAN

Lothrop, Lee & Shepard Books
New York

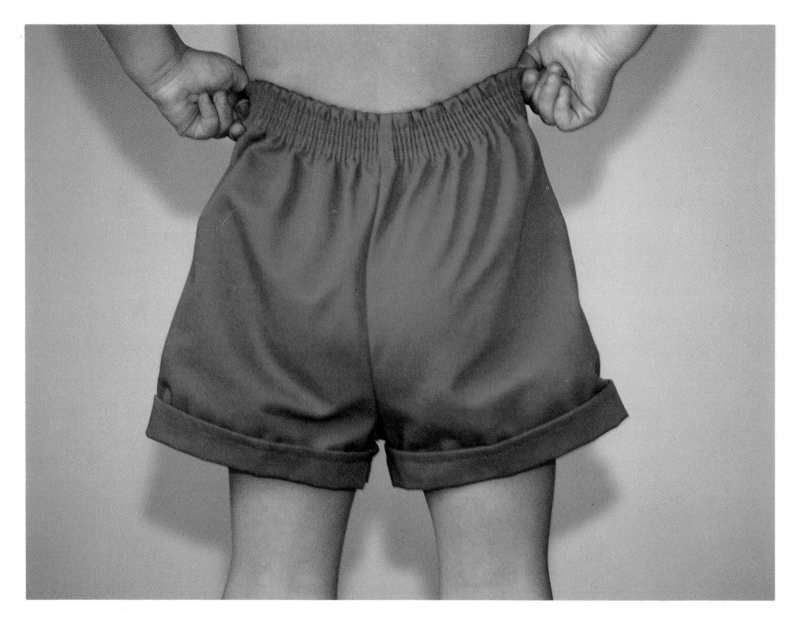

Bottom

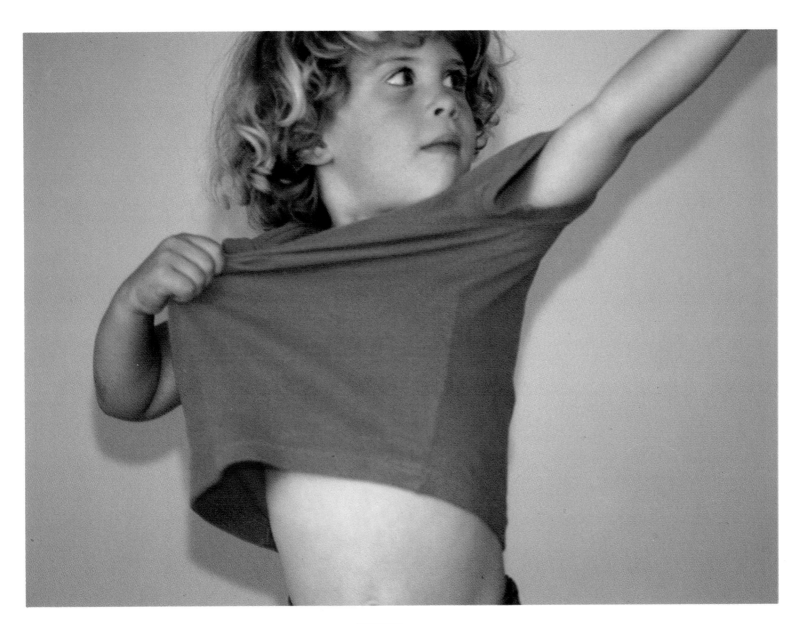

Top

Above

Below

Whole

Half

Full

Empty

Backward

Frontward

Small

Big

In back

In front

Far

Near

Narrow

Wide

Same

Different

Many

Few

None

About This Book

I first met Becca (Rebecca Massanari) when she was one day old. She and I are good buddies, so it was a treat for me to photograph her for this book. All the photographs were taken at the Massanari farm in Springvale, Maine. Becca's older sister and brother, Jessica and Derrek Massanari, were able assistants. Becca's parents, Dave and Nancy Massanari, were patient, helpful, and understanding. Without them this book would not have been possible, and I am forever grateful to them.

The photographs were taken with a Nikon F2 and FE2 camera, with Nikkor lenses. The lighting was a mix of available light, sunlight reflector fill, and bare-bulb electronic flash. Kodachrome 64 film was used, and the processing was done by Kodak.

428
M   McMillan, Bruce

      Be   ackward,
        Becca frontward

         $11.8

428
M   McMillan, Bruce

          Becca backward,
           Becca frontward

      $11.88

DATE	BORROWER'S NAME	